# FROM DESERTS
## *to Gardens*

# FROM DESERTS
## *to Gardens*

A COLLECTION OF
BREATH, BLOOMS, AND LIGHT.

**MEL MARIE**

RESOURCE *Publications* · Eugene, Oregon

**FROM THE AUTHOR**

THIS IS A COLLECTION FROM MY HEART. I HAVE ALWAYS BEEN SMITTEN OVER LANGUAGE AND POETRY. OVER THE YEARS, I HAVE QUIETLY KEPT MUCH OF IT CLOSE TO ME OR I WOULD EXPRESS IT THROUGH MY YOGA TEACHING. YOGA TEACHING FOR ME IS AN ART, A CANVAS FOR LANGUAGE TO LAND AND TRANSCEND. I WANT TO THANK MY STUDENTS FOR WRAPPING ME IN BRAVERY AND LOVE TO SHARE MY HEART. AND ALL OF THOSE WHO HAVE BROKE MY HEART, NURSED MY HEART, AND AWAKENED MY HEART- THANK YOU.

MAY THESE WORDS BE A MIRROR INTO THE HUMAN OF YOU. A BREATH OF FRESH AIR, A HOME TO CUDDLE IN, COURAGE TO RESIDE IN.

THE TITLE 'FROM DESERTS TO GARDENS' CAME FROM ISAIAH 51:3

"FOR THE LORD COMFORTS ZION; HE COMFORTS ALL HER WASTE PLACES AND MAKES HER WILDERNESS LIKE EDEN, HER DESERT LIKE THE GARDEN OF THE LORD; JOY AND GLADNESS WILL BE FOUND IN HER, THANKSGIVING AND THE VOICE OF SONG."

MAY THIS ANTHOLOGY BE A SPACE WHERE THE POETRY BECOMES A PRACTICE. SOMETHING COZY, SAVORING AND REAL.

MAY THIS BOOK BE AN EXPERIENCE FOR THE HEART:
TO GROW, HEAL, AND BLOOM INTO THE GARDEN OF YOU.

FOR IYLA MARIE
BE BRAVE. YOU ARE MADE OF MOON.

**HOW TO NAVIGATE THIS BOOK**

POETRY HAS TRADITIONALLY BEEN A MEANS OF SHARED EXPRESSION AIDING IN THE PROCESS OF RECOVERY AND RELEASE. THIS MODALITY OF LANGUAGE IS A FORM OF NARRATIVE HEALING OFFERING SPACE AND MEDICINE THROUGH HONEST CONNECTION AND THOUGHTFUL INQUIRY. THIS PRACTICE OF NARRATIVE PSYCHOLOGY PRESERVES HUMAN-NESS, EVOKES POST-TRAUMATIC GROWTH, ELICITS SELF-UNDERSTANDING WHILE AWAKENING YOU FROM THE INSIDE OUT.

I WANTED TO CREATE AN INTERACTIVE ANTHOLOGY THAT CALLS YOU TO SHOW UP AND PARTICIPATE IN YOUR EXPERIENCE. THIS IS MINDFULNESS, THE ESSENCE OF YOGA, THE ESSENCE OF SELF CARE. STUDIES HAVE SHOWN THAT WHEN TWO PEOPLE READ OR EXPLORE POETRY AND MEANINGFUL NARRATIVES TOGETHER, COUPLING IN BRAIN ACTIVITY OCCURS, NUEROPLASTICITY IS INDUCED, HEART RATE CHANGES, AND WE BEGIN TO ENGENDER ACCOMMODATIVE PROCESSING.

THIS JOURNAL IS A SELF CARE KEEPSAKE. A SPACE WHERE YOU NOTE YOUR YES'S AND NO'S. PRAYER IN INK. LAUGHTER OUT LOUD. PAUSES- WHERE YOU FEEL THE EARTH BENEATH YOU AND LOVE AROUND YOU. TO TUNE IN AND UNCOVER AGAIN AND AGAIN. AN INVITATION TO BEFRIEND THE INSIDE DEEPER PARTS OF YOUR HEART. SOOTHE, CALM AND ALIGN INTO THE PRESENT MOMENT. THIS IS THE PRACTICE OF POETRY. TO TASTE IT BEYOND THOUGHT AND ALLOW THE PROCESS TO WORK THROUGH YOU, CHANGE YOU AND CALL YOU TO WRITE BACK.

I INVITE YOU TO FILL OUT THE JOURNAL PROMPTS, TO USE THIS TO INSPIRE YOUR ARTICULATION- YOUR OWN ART. MAYBE YOU NEED SOMETHING TO
LANGUAGE YOUR YOGA CLASS OR ADD TO A LOVE LETTER. MAYBE IT BECOMES THE CATALYST FOR YOUR MANTRA, MAKE IT YOURS.

EVERY TIME YOU SEE THIS LOTUS BUD ON A PAGE, YOU WILL KNOW THE PAGE IS AN INVITATION FOR INQUIRY.

PLAY. NEGOTIATE WITH THE NARRATIVES. BREATHE.
THIS IS THE PRACTICE OF POETRY.

INTEGRITY IS
THE STEM OF
ALL THAT
BLOOMS.

SO STOP
DIGGING INTO
YOUR GARDEN
OF WOUNDS.

TO OPEN, YET
ROOT- THE
RIDDLE OF
YOU.

FROM
DESERTS TO
GARDENS,
THIS GARDEN
FOR YOU.

WITHOUT THE CARICATURE OF MY WORDS
MY MEMORY OF HIM WOULD BE VAGUE.
AND WISHFUL.

I HOLD OUR STORIES BETWEEN MY HANDS
CAPTURING EVERY VALLEY AND SEA
OF HIM IN INK.

BREATH AND LONGING.
TO RETURN AND STAY WHERE OUR HEARTS
DIDN'T FEEL SO TIRED.

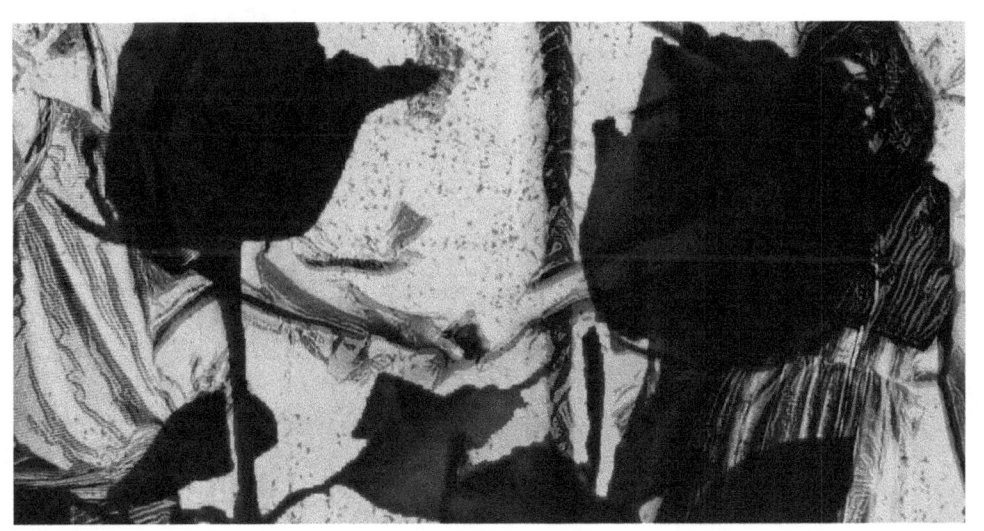

HOW COULD I TREAD
THE SURFACE OF YOU
WHEN I'VE
ALREADY TASTED
THE LAYERS,
THE DIMENSIONS
AND GALAXIES OF YOU.

DON'T CAGE ME IN
YOUR POOL WHEN I
KNOW THERE ARE
OCEANS TO YOU.

I LIVE INSIDE A RAINDROP.

IT FALLS AND

FALLS AND

FALLS.

WAITING FOR PAVEMENT.

WHILE TRAVELING DOWN- MY RAINDROP LIFE THINS UNTIL THE EXPERIENCE OF THE FALL HAS STRIPPED ME DRY.


        -TRUSTING YOU

**NEWS ON DEPLOYMENT:**
MY REACTION WAS BROKEN ICE
AND IT WAS FATE THAT DROPPED ME.

YOU HOLD THE UNIVERSE TOGETHER
DESPERATELY KEEPING IT
WRAPPING IT UP WITH REDIRECTION
BACK TO YOUR WAY.

BUT DON'T YOU KNOW
EVENTUALLY THERE WILL BE
A BIG BANG BECAUSE
HISTORY REPEATS ITSELF.
AND EVENTUALLY
YOUR FINGERS WILL BE BURNT
FROM PIECING STARDUST
INTO BLACKHOLES.

EVENTUALLY, THE HOLDING
WILL BECOME CONSUMING,
SWALLOWING YOU UP
INTO CONSTELLATIONS
OF THE SHATTERED AND THE RIGID.

DIDN'T YOU KNOW PLAYING GOD WAS A
BARGAIN WITH THE DARK.

I WILL SET TABLES IN
YOUR WAR.

I WILL STAND THROUGH
YOUR STORM.

I WILL BE THE LIGHTENING
UNDER YOUR SKIN.

THE AFTER. THE WHEN
THIS IS OVER. I WILL.

I GLOOM IN NEGATIVITY AND BLOOM IN SHARING IT WITH YOU.

WE PRACTICE SELF CARE SO WE DO NOT PASS THE SHADOW TO OTHERS. POETRY OFFERS A SAFE SPACE TO HELP US FEEL LESS LONELY AND PROCESS OUR OWN PROCESS OF FLOWING. DID YOU KNOW THAT SCIENCE SHOWS LONELINESS RESONATES IN THE SAME PART OF THE BRAIN AS PHYSICAL PAIN? IT ALSO HAS BEEN LINKED TO POOR HEALTH AND HEART DISEASE.

WHETHER IT BE ON THE YOGA MAT, THROUGH NARRATIVE EXPRESSION OR EVEN IN SPIRITUAL GATHERINGS- WE TRY TO MAKE SENSE OF THE SHADOW. EXPLORE THE CORNERS OF LONELINESS. TAKE A MOMENT AND BREATHE IN THROUGH THE NOSE, AND OUT. WE FEEL IT, THEN FREE IT.

WHAT DO YOU WISH TO LET GO? LIST IT. WRITE IT. DRAW IT.

SOMEONE ONCE SHARED A BEAUTIFUL QUOTE OR CONCEPT; THIS IDEA OF NOT BLEEDING ON THE PEOPLE WHO DIDN'T CUT YOU.

WHAT ARE WAYS YOU CREATE SPACE? WHAT ARE PRACTICES THAT ALLOW YOU TO RELIEVE, RELEASE, AND BREATHE AGAIN?

LIST ANY SELF CARE OR CLEANSING RITUALS YOU PRACTICE? LIST IDEAS OF SELF CARE OR CLEANSING PRACTICES YOU WISH TO START APPLYING.

I LOVE THAT YOU ARE A WOUND.
BECAUSE YOU FADE,
AS I HEAL.

I LIVE THE LIFE OF A ROPE SWING.
A GAMBLE, A DARE
EATING DREAMS LIKE AIR
      STRETCHED AND PULLED BACK
USED AND LEFT IN THE DARK
BUT THE COOL ELEMENTS BELOW PULLS
THE LIGHT FROM MY HEART.

SOMEDAYS FEEL LIKE JUMPING
INTO DARK WATER.
AND I TRY TO REMEMBER
SEEDS HAVE NEVER KNOWN
THE FLOWER, THEY SIMPLY
JUST REMEMBER TO GROW.

YOU DON'T RETIRE WITH YOUR LADY FRIENDS.
YOU SIMPLY RETIRE THEM.

I WILL LET THEM DROP FROM MY FINGERTIPS,
OUR STORIES, SCRIBBLED SEPARATELY.

- HURT FEELINGS

YOU WRAP ME IN HERE AND NOW.

HANDING OVER YOURSELF LIKE
IT'S WHAT YOU KNOW TO DO.

LIKE STARS ALIGNED
AND SENT THIS COMMAND TO YOU.

BUT BE WEARY, HAVEN'T YOU HEARD
I CAN SEE RIGHT THROUGH.

THAT YOU'RE A NAKED MAN
TRYING TO HAND
ME A SHIRT THAT DOESN'T
BELONG TO YOU.

I LEAD WITH MORE HEART THAN HANDS.
I'VE LEARNED TO LOVE THINGS INTO BEING.
THAT ALL THE DETAILS WILL FALL
THROUGH MY FINGERS QUICKER THAN WHEN
KEPT WITHIN THE LOCKET OF MY HEART.

THAT MY HANDS ARE TOO SMALL TO CARRY
ALL THE FRAGMENTS AND FACES.
ALL THE PLACES.

MAYBE THIS IS WHY
GHOSTS DON'T HAUNT HANDS BUT HEARTS.

I AM NO LONGER INTERESTED
IN EXCHANGING MY BONES
FOR YOUR COMFORT.

THESE VERTEBRAE AREN'T
STAIRS FOR YOU TO CLIMB.

MY HEART, NOT A TENT TO
CAMP AND LEAVE.

DON'T APOLOGIZE FOR YOUR TEARS.
FOR EACH DROP HOLDS
WHAT FLOWERS NEED
TO BLOOM.

IF I BELONG ANYWHERE,
I HOPE IT'S IN INK ON YOUR PAGES.

WHERE YOU MAKE SENSE OF THIS HAUNTING.
HOW MY GHOST MADE A HOME IN YOUR DARK.

AND I HOPE YOU REMEMBER ME IN THIS WAY.
HOLDING A LOVING GARDEN FOR YOUR HEART.
A REFUGE FOR YOUR DEEP KEPT THOUGHTS.
A HAUNTING FOR WHEN YOU DON'T.

WE WERE LEFT
HUNGOVER
WITH REGRET
TO SEARCH
FOR THE
PIECES YOU
STOLE THAT
NIGHT.
AND WITH IT
ALL THE
SORRIES I
EVER HAD
FELL OFF LIKE
EYELASHES
TWISTED AND
SAD.

LET ME LEAVE YOU WITH FRESH BREATH
AND A WATERED SOUL.

AWAKENED INTIMATELY AND FULL
AS THOUGH, THE GARDEN IN YOU
DRANK UP MY LIGHT.
AND THE COLORS OF YOU-
FIERCE, IGNITE.

LET ME PLANT IN YOU
A FIELD OF STRENGTH.
WILDFLOWERS AND MIRRORS,
TRANSCENDING THE PAIN

LIKE A WOMB AND LABOR,
MY LABOR OF LOVE.
ALWAYS KNOW YOU ARE GOOD ENOUGH.

SHE TRACES MEMORIES
WITH HER HEART
OUTLINING THE DETAILS
SPACIOUS AND ALWAYS
MORE ENCHANTING
THAN IT ACTUALLY IS.

THE FUTURE IS OVER THE MOUNTAIN.

NARRATIVE HEALING EMOTES THE BREADTH OF THE HUMAN EXPERIENCE ILLUMINATING A SPECTRUM OF POSSIBILITY. IT PLANTS US INTO THE CLARITY THAT PROVOKES OUR CONFIDENCE TO GO IN AND FORTH. THROUGH THIS EFFORT, WE BEGIN TO YEILD A PSYCHOLOGICAL WEB OF MULTIFACETED EXPRESSION THAT RESONATES AND CONNECTS US DEEPER TO ONE ANOTHER.

HOW DO YOU WANT TO FEEL RIGHT NOW?

*LIST YOUR FAVORITE WORDS*

UNDERSTAND ME
THE WAY SOIL KNOWS ENTELECHY.
THE WAY IT ACTIVATES GROWTH
SIMULTANEOUS TO
HOLDING A HOME.

STILLNESS FEELS LIKE NOTHING. AND WHEN WE PAUSE WITH SUCH DELIBERATE PURPOSE- I REALIZE I DO NOT BELONG IN MY FLESH.

OR EVEN BESIDE IT.

-FIRST TIME MEDITATING

I AM NOT A BRIDGE TO BE LITTERED ON,
A PATH FOR YOU TO WALK THROUGH.
I RAISE CITIES WITH MY TONGUE,
FLOWERS FROM FORGOTTEN DREAMS.
I PLANT HOPE IN DESOLATE SPACES AND
TAKE TIME WITH DELICATE THINGS.

BUT LITTER ON MY BRIDGE, STEAL MY
FLOWERS, ABLAZE MY TREES-
THE STRENGTH OF MY STRUCTURE
WILL COLLAPSE BENEATH YOURR FEET.

WHY IS IT FRUSTRATION IGNITES MY ATTRACTION.
I HOLD AN OCCUPATION OF FIXING IT.

HE TAKES MY BREATH
AND PULLS ME UNDER-

HOW LOVABLE I AM, WHEN HE IS NOT.
HOW LOVABLE IS HE, WHEN I AM NOT.

**ALLOW IT TO BECOME,**

**YOUR SPIRITUAL TEACHER.**

WHAT HAPPENS WHEN YOU ALLOW THE EXPERIENCE, HIM, HER, THAT *THING*- TO BECOME YOUR SPIRITUAL TEACHER?
WHAT ARE YOU LEARNING ABOUT YOURSELF THROUGH THIS SPIRITUAL TEACHER?
HOW ARE YOU GROWING?

TRYING TO REPLACE THE COURAGE LOST
INSIDE OF YOU.

AS YOU DERAIL-
SPILLING YOURSELF ACROSS
THE COUNTERTOP OF MY HEART,
CONTEMPLATING WHETHER A DEATH SLOW
AND PREPARED LEAVES LESS DESTRUCTION
THAN AN UNEXPECTED INSTANT TEAR.

WHAT IS DEATH OTHER THAN AN UNFOLDING.
I DON'T THINK THERE IS FEAR IN NOT
KNOWING, OTHER THAN THE GRAVEYARD OF
LEFTOVER YOU. THINKING I WAS HEALING BY
BURYING MY COURAGE IN YOU.

IT BEGAN AS THOUGH I
BLOOMED IN YOUR PALMS,

BUT PICKED FLOWERS ALWAYS DIE.

A BLINK AWAY, AS DUTY CALLS
AND I THINK HOW AFGHANISTAN IS
ONE LUCKY COUNTRY TO POSSESS
THE PRESENCE OF YOU.

MAYBE IT'LL BECOME ALIVE
WITH LIGHT THE WAY I DO
WHEN I AM WITH YOU.

ALL THE SUNRISES ON YOUR PALMS
SONGS YOU SING THROUGH ME
INDEED, YOU'RE TANTALIZING CUISINE
UNTIL I DIGEST
          YOUR MESS
               I WILL CLEAN
OBSCENE, I WILL PURIFY
ALL THE SUNSETS IN YOUR PALMS
YOU CALM, HOLDING MY HEART IN YOUR
TEETH BENEATH YOU ARE THEIR
MALADIES, TRAGEDIES, I WAIT FOR YOU
UNTIL YOU RETURN TO ME.

FRESH KISS OF AUTUMN
SOFTEN MY FLESH
AND FLESH, I SINK TO THE
BOTTOM GROUNDED IN THIS
MESS.
POOLS OF CIGARETTE BUTTS
CHANGE, WRAPPERS AND GHOSTS
CORRESCATED SPIRIT GUTS
IN THIS TOWN I LOVE MOST.

-ASHEVILLE

OUR LOVE FEELS LIKE A JUMP ROPE
OUT OF BREATH
CHALLENGING TO SYNC
EASY TO TRIP
BUT ALWAYS CALLING ME.

HMM BONES, ANKLEBONES AND BONES
AND FOSSA OF TUMBLING TUBEROSITIES
OF CITIES LIVING IN ME,

A FAÇADE OF CARNAL VULNERABILITY.
STIMULATE ME,
WITH THE PSYCHOLOGY OF NEURONS
AND MIRROR NEURONS INTIMATELY.

REFUTE ALL THE POET'S TRAUMATIC ADVERSITY.
NURTURE ME, WITH THE MUSICAL THREAD CLICKING
METRONOME ONLY MEASURING TIME
WITH YOUR BODY AND MINE.

DELICATELY, YOU SPILL RAINBOWS
FROM YOUR EYELIDS AS YOU SURVEY MY BODY.
MY LOVE IS A POEM, YOU AND I, ALONE WHISPERING
THE SECRETS OF PHYSICAL CADENCES
THAT YOU CALL CIRCLES.
AND THE CIRCLES ARE NOW CIRCLING ME.

THE CIRCUMFERENCE OF INFINITY,
THIS MEMORY,
THIS LOVE, VULNERABILITY.

I'M PITCHING
TENTS ON
YOUR ROCKY
SPINE
I CAN FIND
A HOME
IN YOU
EVEN IF
IT'S ONLY
FOR NOW
I AM AT HOME
IN YOU.

OBSERVING TIME THROUGH THE EYES
OF NATURE AND ATOMPSHERIC CONDITIONS-
HOW WELL CONNECTED
THE ANCIENTS WERE TO PRESENCE.

NOW, WE'VE BECOME SWALLOWED UP
BY MAN MADE MEASUREMENTS,
MINDED AWAY BY THE REVELATIONS
OUTSIDE OUR WINDOWS.

WE HAVE LOCKED OURSELVES IN.
WHO REALLY KNOWS WHAT IS IN.

I WILL UNCOVER YOU
IN LACED WRAPPED MEMORIES
OF ILLUSION AND EASY
BECAUSE THINGS ARE NEVER EASY
AND ILLUSIONS WILL ALWAYS BE ILLUSION.

SO DESIRABLE,
TASTY
AND SAFE.

LIKE VIBRANT STARS FLOW
CALLING ME TO DREAM
BUT THEY ARE ALL DEAD.
IS IT EVEN WHAT IT SEEMS?

**THE EGO FEEDS OFF OF OUR ILLUSIONS.**

**IT DRINKS UP THE ATTACHMENT NARRATIVE THAT SOMETHING BELONGS TO US OR IS ENTITLED TO US- GIVING BIRTH TO THE MOST PAINFUL LONGINGS AND THE ANCHOR OF ISOLATION. IN SOME CASES IT FEEDS OUR SEPARATION NARRATIVE THAT WE ARE BETTER THAN THEM OR SEPARATE OR LESS THAN. THE EGO AIDS IN SPIRITUAL IGNORANCE AND FACILITIES THE DANCE OF LONELINESS. THESE 'TRUTHS' ABOUT EGO CALL THE NEED TO DEVELOP A WITNESSER PRACTICE. TO SEE THE PAIN, THE HURT. TO GET CLOSE TO IT AND FEEL THE REALNESS OF THE STORY.**

**WE MUST THEN BEGIN THE PROCESS OF DEBUNKING, DIFFUSING, VENTILATING, RELEASING.**

FEEL IT | WRITE IT OUT | WHAT IS YOUR SIDE OF THE STORY

WHY DOES IT
MATTER | WHAT
CAN THEY DO TO
MAKE IT BETTER |
WHAT WOULD
NEED TO HAPPEN
TO MAKE IT
BETTER?








SEE IT FROM THE
OUTSIDE. WHAT DOES
THE EGO SAY? GIVE IT
PERMISSION TO
DISSOLVE | SIT IN
YOUR CENTER,
UNMOVED.

HE ASKED ME WHAT IT WAS THAT I
WRITE ABOUT...
MY RESPONSE?

THE UNCONTROLLED IMPULSIONS
THAT LIGHT UP LIKE FIREFLIES IN
MY HEAD. I TRY TO CATCH THEM
AND WRITE THEM DOWN BEFORE
THEY FADE AWAY, YA KNOW?

I KNOW.

LIKE A LOCKET, YOU OPEN ME
SNUGGLED CLOSE INTIMATELY
THIS LOCKET LEFT
OPEN TO RUST
LEFT ME RUSTING
IN THE DUST.

LAUGHING EYES
ENCOURAGED ME
"MY DEAR YOU HAVE
THE WORLD TO SEE
NOT MANY ARE AS LOVELY
AS YOU
NOT MANY CARRY
AS MUCH VALUE.
LIKE IGNORING GOLD AND
CHOOSING METAL
DON'T YOU DARE BEGIN TO
SETTLE."
LAUGHING EYES
YOUR WORDS ARE SWEET
HELPING ME
WHEN I CAN'T BREATHE.

AT NINETEEN
YOU WOULD ASSUME,
I WOULDN'T PERISH
AS I BLOOM.

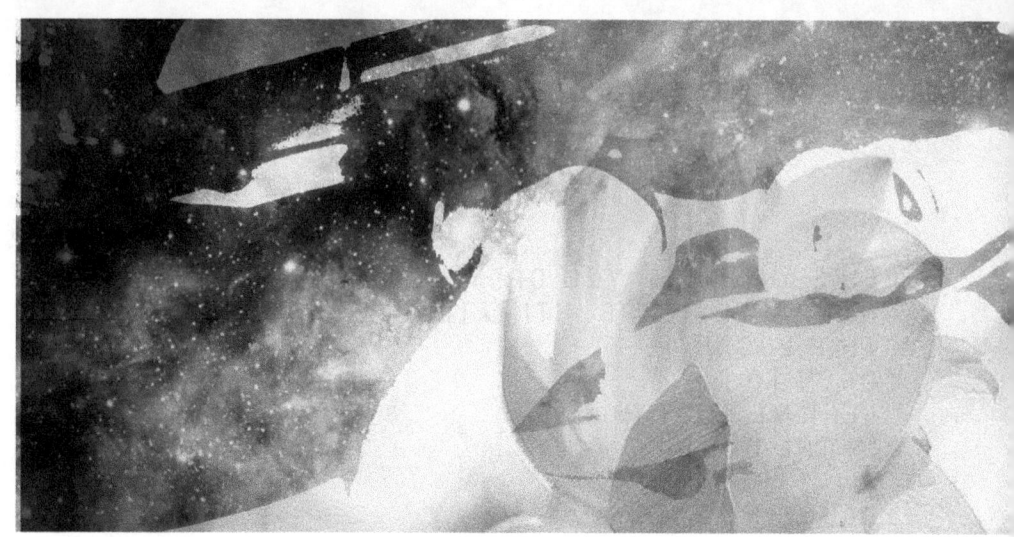

I TASTE YOU IN COCA-COLA, COOKIE DOUGH AND
HONEYSUCKLES. YOU ARE LAUGHTER,
CRUMPLED WARMTH IN SLEPT IN CLOTHES.
HAYDEN, I SEE YOU IN SLEEPING BAGS,
TEAR KITS AND ROLLERBLADES.
I HEAR YOU IN PLUCKED GUITAR STRINGS,
CAMERA SHUTTERS AND POPPED KNUCKLES.

YOU ARE LAUGHTER, CRUMPLED WARMTH
IN SLEPT IN CLOTHES. I FEEL YOU
IN SPIRIT FINGERS, SWIMMING POOLS
AND INTERVENTIONS. HAYDEN, I HEAR YOU
IN PLUCKED GUITAR STRINGS,
CAMERA SHUTTERS AND POPPED KNUCKLES.
YOU ARE ANCHOR HEAVY ON MY HEART.

I FEEL YOU IN SPIRIT FINGERS, SWIMMING POOLS
AND INTERVENTIONS. YOU ARE CRUMBLING
RED ROSES AND CAR CRASHES. HAYDEN,
I TASTE YOU IN COCA-COLA, COOKIE DOUGH
AND HONEYSUCKLES. YOU ARE GHOST,
WRITTEN LOVE ON MY HEART.

I FEEL LIKE AN 8 BALL.
PASSED AND PASSED
ONLY TO SEE
WHO IS GOING TO BE
LUCKY WITH ME.

**BE KIND** TO YOUR HEALING. YOU HEAL BECAUSE YOU ARE ALIVE, YOU'RE ALIVE BECAUSE YOU HEAL.

**BE KIND** TO THE FEELINGS. YOU FEEL BECAUSE YOU ARE REAL, YOU ARE REAL BECAUSE YOU HEAL.

I HATE LETTING GO

    DISMISSIVE AT BEST
        AGONIZING AT WORST

IF I COULD BUNDLE IT ALL UP
PACK IT IN A PLACE
RATHER THAN THROW IT AWAY
BECAUSE NIGHTS LIKE THESE
RETURNING FEELS SO SAFE.

YOU CAN'T PLUCK YOUR OWN PETALS,
AND THEN WISH TO BLOOM.

YOU ARE A SACRED CONTAINER OF LIGHT
A NOURISHER OF MOUNTAINS
WITH THE STRENGTH
OF A SUNRISE.

& FOR HER,
YOU WILL ALWAYS FEEL LIKE SUN-
HOLDING LIGHT TO THE GALAXIES
AND WARMTH ON EVERY COLD DAY.

AS SHE BLOOMS IN YOUR HANDS,
YOU COULD NEVER UNDERSTAND
WHAT BLOOMS IN THIS MOTHER'S HEART.

YOU BRING LIFE TO ME.

WHEN WE ARE TOGETHER,
EVERYTHING ELSE BECOMES NOISE.

YOUR EYES ARE
 PARADOX.

YOU ARE HERE
 AND NOW,
BUT I GAZE
AND RECOGNIZE
 COUNTLESS
MOONS IN YOU.

MEMORIES WRITTEN
ON YOUR SKIN,
YOU HERE
ALL AT ONCE
AND INTIMATELY
YOU.

ALL AT ONCE.

CAN I BE CONTENT KNOWING
I HELD YOUR WORLD FOR MOMENTS.
TO TREASURE THE CAPACITY
OF SOMETHING DIFFERENT
SITTING AT THE EDGE
WONDERING HOW LONG
THE FALL WOULD BE.
MEASURED IN BREATHS?
MOMENTS? THE FALL
WOULD PASS, BUT MY HEART
BECOMES TRAPPED IN THE FOREVER.

FOR MY HEART KNOWS NO MODERATION.
MY HEART DOES THE DEEP DIVE IN,
WHOLE HEARTED AND GONE.

I MET HER LAST NIGHT
THROUGH THE HUM OF BREATH
UNITED.

RECIEVING EACH ELEMENT
CONNECTED.

EXPERIENCING MYSELF,
WHO I AM
A UNIQUE EXPRESSION.

THE TWISTS AND CONTOURS OF MY BODY,
LAID OUT ON THIS MAT.
NO LONGER CHASING-
BUT ALLOWING THIS,
THIS HEART TO REST.

I MET HER LAST NIGHT
I FELL IN LOVE WITH HER BREATH.

YOGA IS...

THE UNION OF MIND, BODY AND BREATH.
AN EXEMPLIFICATION OF PRESENCE. NOT PERFORMANCE
OR PHYSICAL ACCOMPLISHMENT. JUST PRESENCE,
EXPERIENCE, PSYCHO-SOMATIC EMBODIMENT.

YOGA IS A TECHNOLOGY FOR WELLNESS, EVERYTHING
ELSE IS JUST AN EXPRESSION OF SOMEONE
ELSES'S INDIVIDUAL PRACTICE. GROUND INTO YOURS,
TAKE INQUIRY AND TUNE INTO YOUR OWN EXPRESSION.

MINDFUL MOVEMENT, SOMATIC INTEGRATION, SELF CARE,
MEDITATIVE STRETCHING- IT'S YOUR YOGA. ALLOW YOGA
TO BE A PLAYGROUND OF INQUIRY. THIS IS
YOUR PRACTICE OFF THE MAT AND BACK TO THE MAT.

**WHAT DOES IT MEAN TO BE EMBODIED?
WHAT ARE WAYS YOU DISCOVER PRESENCE?**

I THINK PEOPLE ENJOY PAIN
BECAUSE WE LIVE IN A WORLD
TOO FAST TO FEEL.

SO WE LONG FOR SENSATION KNOWING,
BROKEN HEARTS FEEL LIKE SOMETHING.

I WANT TO SPONGE YOUR HEARTACH
WRING IT OUT TO THE SEA
HOPING NATURE WILL FILTER THE PAIN
LIKE YOU HAD DONE FOR ME.

YOUR COLD

TEACHES ME

MY WARMTH

BEING IN LOVE IS
VIBRANT, SECURE.
SOFT WIND TO TOUCH.
PERFECT CHAI,
CRYSTALS AND SUNLIGHT.

DIM LIGHT, PILLOW TALK.
THE WAY WE SPEAK IN *COME HERE*.

I PAINT WITH MY WORDS
      AND MY IMPRESSION-

A CANVAS ON YOUR HEART.

ASKING FOR HELP
DOESN'T MEAN
YOU ARE WEAK.

FOR THIS IS
THE LANGUAGE
OF COURAGE.

AFFIRMATION
THAT YOU
ARE STRONGER
THAN YOUR EGO.

I AM A MAGNET
BURNING THROUGH YOUR HEART.
LIVING IN TRIANGLES
COMPLEX AND SHARP.

YOU DRANK THE RIVER
DRY TO STONE.
AND YOU WONDER WHY
YOU WANDER ALONE.

I AM A MAGNET
BURNING YOUR HEART.
BECAUSE I AM LIGHT
THAT EXPOSED YOUR DARK.

I KNOW THE STORMS I BRING OUT OF PEOPLE.

AND THE FLOWERS THAT BLOOM FROM IT.

COLORS WILL ALWAYS BLEED THROUGH,
ESPECAILLY WHEN THE PAINTING
HAS BEEN DRENCHED WITH ABUSE.

YOU CAN TRY AND PEEL,
COPY AND USE.
BUT EVERYONE KNOWS
THAT IT'S JUST YOU.

YOU CAN CAST YOUR HOOK
INTO THE SEA
SEARCHING FOR WAYS
TO CATCH HOLD OF ME.

TO DROWN AND SCARE
YOU DARKNESS, YOU SHREW
BUT I HAVE LEARNED TO RISE,
**I AM UNMOVED.**

TODAY'S SURRENDER
IS TOMORROWS PEACE.

PEOPLE HURT US
AND WE BLAME GOD.
AS THOUGH THIS ACCUSATION GIVES THE
FREEDOM FROM ACCOUNTABILITY.

THE FREEDOM TO
THROW OUR HANDS TO THE SKY,
OUR HEARTS TO THE DIRT
THINKING IF IT WASN'T FOR GOD
THIS WOULDN'T HURT.

BUT WE'VE MUDDIED TRUTH,
PLACING PEOPLE INTO THE TEMPLE BECAUSE
SATAN KNOWS
THAT HUMAN TRUST
IS AN ALLY OF THE DEVIL.

**HAYDEN AND LYNDSEY**

QUIETLY, I KEEP YOU CLOSE.
IN WHISPERS
YOU SPEAK TO ME.
IN EXHALES YOU THEN LEAVE.
YOU ARE WIND IN THE TREES.

CANDLE LIGHT, CANDLE SCENT
CANDLES WHISPER DON'T RESENT.

BECAUSE DIM LIGHT POURS OUT QUIET,
UNTIL ILLUMINATION CAUSES RIOT.

- THAT OVER THINKING

WHEN DID YOU MAKE
A FLASK OUT OF MY HEART.

HIDING HER IN YOU POCKETS
AND FORGOTTEN CABINETS.
LID HALFWAY LOOSE,
AVAILABLE AND USED.
WHOLEHEARTEDLY HERE,
WAITING FOR YOU.

DO I TASTE LIKE RAIN
OR SUMMERTIME SAD.
A SHOT OF ME BRAVE,
SOMETHING DANGEROUS AND BAD.

OR IS IT THE WAY I ALLOW
YOUR BREATH TO REST,
AS TEARS RAIN DOWN YOUR SELFISH CHEST.

HER CAPE IS MADE FROM SELF LOVE.
SHE STANDS ON THE GROUND
OF AFFIRMATION
STRENGTH
AND FEMININE.

AVAILABLE FOR A GARDEN
TO AWAKEN,
LIGHT TO BE PLANTED
AND BRAVE TO HOLD RAIN IN.

SHE KNOWS THAT THE RECIPE OF
DARK BEGINS WITH TOO MUCH BRIGHT
SO SHE GIVES HERSELF THE PERMISSION
TO BE HUMAN.

A PRACTICE OF SOFT
SHOWING UP FOR THE NIGHT.

YOUR WORDS
ARE A RESTING HOME.

MY TIRED HEART
FINDS HOME
IN THE LANGUAGE OF YOU.

A FLOWER OPENS ITSELF INTO LIGHT, ROOTS ITSELF INTO DARK AND RENDERS CLEAR FOR NOURISHMENT.

THE FLOWER IS A POEM OF BOTH STRONG AND SOFT. PARADOX OF EXPRESSION. A CAROUSEL OF COLOR.

MOVEMENT,
BREATH,
AND STILLNESS.
SUBTLE TO HOLD.

IT TAKES TIME TO BLOOM.
IT TAKES TIME TO BECOME.

BREATHE IN GRACE.
IT'S THE KINDEST BREATH
YOU'LL TAKE.

**VULNERABILITY**

SOME SAY WE BEND
SO WE DON'T BREAK.

I BEND TO BREAK OPEN
AGAIN AND AGAIN
DIFFERENTLY,
WHOLEHEARTEDLY.

LIKE A MIRROR
TO THE MOON,
I FIND WAYS
TO LET MY LIGHT BREATHE.

YOU THINK I BLEED,
BUT THIS IS HOW I BREATHE.

I'M NOT YOUR BUTTERFLY
THESE ARE MY WINGS.

AND THIS, MY COCOON
A COFFIN TO YOU.
BECAUSE I SHED THE LAYERS THAT
KEPT ME CONFUSED.

PUT TO DEATH MY FEAR
NO LONGER PRISONER OF YOU.

FORWARD FOLD INTO ME
A LULLABY AS I BREATHE

STRETCH YOUR SOUL

    YOUR MIND

        ALL THREE

UNTIL YOU BEND BACK INTO ME.

I FIND LOVE IN THE PALMS OF HER HANDS.
THE LITTLE LINES AND FINGERS
MAPPING EVERY HEARTBEAT PRAYER.
THE QUIET MOTIVATIONS TO MY MORNING,
DRESSED UP SUNDAY MORNINGS OR COZIED IN LAYERS
OF LAUGHTER THAT MAKE THE FOUNDATIONS OF ANY HOME.
IN THE SOFTNESS OF HER BREATH, I COULD NEVER FEEL ALONE

POETRY IN MOONLIGHT EYES.
LULLABY IN HER LILY PAD SENTENCES.
THE HARMONY HUMMING SOFTNESS
INTO MY RIGID KNEES, TIRED FEET, AND FENCES.
TENDERNESS IN COMPLETION BECAUSE SHE KNOWS
NO OTHER WAY. PURPOSE AND MAGIC BEYOND WHAT
WORDS WOULD CONVEY.
COULDN'T QUANTIFY THIS LOVE,
NOT EVEN BEACHES FULL OF SAND.
PEOPLE SEEK ANSWERS IN DIVERSE VENTURES
ALL SO CALCULATED AND PLANNED-

ALL THIS MEANING THEY'VE SEARCHED FOR,
I HAVE FOUND IN HER LITTLE HAND.

I KNOW THE WEAPON OF YOUR LIES
WHERE WOLVES EAT THROUGH YOUR EYES.

AND THE WEAPON OF
YOUR LIPS
YOUR JAW.

IT'S YOU WHO'S UNWISE.

THE EPITOME OF
GROUNDING, GROUNDING
DOWN FROM TADASANA.
TADASANA
SHADOWING OVER ME
DELINEATING TREE BRANCH
LIMB INTENDING,
INTENTION
TO BREATHE. RELEASE AND
MELT DOWN,
GROUND THROUGH MY
STICKY RUBBER HUE.
CONTINUE, UNRAVELING
LIKE A BALL
OF YARN. START STRING BY
STRING GENTLY PULL, NO
RIPPING. BREATH BY
BREATH AND HOLD
STRIPPING THE TIES OF
TIME AND MONKEY MIND.
UNWIND, WATERFALLING
SADNESS FROM YOUR EYES.
INTERNALIZE. EXPERIENCE
EACH SENSATION
EMANCIPATION OM MANE
PADME HUM HUM HUM THE
BEATING OF YOUR HEART.
DEPART PAST, DEPART
FUTURE. INHALE HERE,
YOUR INNER MIRROR.
SOMETHING BEAUTIFUL.
THE EXHALE OF EMOTIONAL FREEDOM. SOMETHING
BEAUTIFUL THE EXHALE, THE LAST SOMETHING
BEAUTIFUL YOUR BODY WILL EVER DO. AND BENEATH
YOU, I HOLD YOU. YOUR FOOT PRINTS MESHED IN ME,
FINGER PADS ADDING GRIP, STABLE, MOBILITY, JAYA
THE YAMAS YOU CHANT OVER ME. SAMSKARA,
SINKING, PAUSE THAT THINKING DEEPENING YOUR
BREATHING, BEING. JUST BEING AND I, YOUR VEHICLE
TO SAFETY YOU TAKE ME TO CLASS, TO HOME, TO
CARPETS, TO MOUNTAINS, TO LAKES, PLACES ALIVE
YOUR MAGIC CARPET RIDE, YOUR SAFE PLACE TO HIDE.

-YOGA MAT

I WANT TO HOLD YOU

LIKE DEEP BREATHS.

DON'T YOU KNOW YOU'RE ENOUGH.
AND YOGA DOES WHAT YOGA DOES.

LAY OUT YOUR MAT,
YOUR FEARS WHATEVERS LEFT
HAND OVER THE POISON
OF TRYING TO BE THE BEST.

ALL THE JUDGEMENT YOU CARRY IN YOUR KNEES
COME AS YOU ARE, YOU CAN BREATHE.
JUST SHOW UP AND TRUST BECAUSE
YOGA DOES WHAT YOGA DOES.

UNFOLD INTO NEW TERRITORY OF
THOUGHT BLOWING KISSES AT THE MOON.

WE HARVEST IT ALL HERE,
ALLOWING OUR BONES TO MELT INTO
SILVER LININGS AND LOVE.

WE RELEASE IT ALL HERE.
RELIEF AS I REST AGAINST THE CHEEK OF GOD.

HOW DO YOU LIVE LIKE YOU PRACTICE?

## HOW DO YOU EMANATE YOUR PRAYER?

HOW DO YOU EMANATE YOUR PRAYER?

I'D RATHER BE A PLANTER
THAN A BUILDER.

ALTHOUGH BOTH ENDURE
STORMS AND SEASONS-

ONE NEVER STOPS GROWING.

"MUTUALITY IS SECURITY."
-SHADOW

THIS OCEAN OF YOU,
HAS MADE CONTINENTS OUT OF ME.

YOUR WAVES TRACING NEW TERRITORY.

CHANGING THE SHORELINES OF MY MIND.
SUCKED IN BY YOUR TSUNAMIS.

UNSURE IF THE WEIGHT-
IS BECAUSE I HOLD ON
OR RESIST THE DROWNING.

RECEIVE ME THE WAY THE
EARTH RECEIVES THE RAIN.

THIRSTY, OPEN AND
READY FOR GROWTH.

I FEEL TANGLED.
MY HEART
OVERSTRETCHED.
THE PIECES
UNRAVELING INTO THIS WEB.

I SEE YOU
WATCHING ME,
WORK MY WAY IN.

AND **FROM THE DISTANCE**
YOU STAND-
I KNOW THE WEB
IS BRILLIANT PATTERNED.
FROM THE DISTANCE,
IT SEEMS I AM HARD AT WORK
FOR YOU TO ENJOY
FROM THE DISTANCE,
YOU ARE SATISFIED
COMPLETELY UNAWARE
THAT I AM TANGLED.

I MISS THE MOONS IN YOUR EYES.
WHEN DID WE GO DIM.
I MISS THE MOON IN OUR SKY, HOW'D
THIS SHADOW GET IN.

GIVE ME TIME.
PATCHING UP THE DAMS
YOU BROKE THROUGH.
THE CLEAN UP, THE COMEDOWN,
ALL THE POEMS I WROTE YOU.

THE NO MORES, THE SPACES,
SEPIA SCENES.
I AM LETTING GO OF YOU
SO I CAN HOLD ONTO ME.

YOU WERE WORMWOOD IN DISGUISE.
I THOUGHT THE TERRITORIES YOU CALLED ME TO
WERE GARDENS AND THE WATER WAS PURE.
I THOUGHT YOUR HANDS WERE GENTLE
AND YOUR LIPS OF HONEY. I WANDERED
DOWN YOUR PATHS AND THROUGH YOUR TERRAINS
LIKE IT WAS THE ARCHITECTURE TO JOY.
I FOLLOWED. WHEN YOU ASKED FOR MORE
OF ME, I UNZIPPED MY HEART AND PULLED BACK
EVERY LAYER. YOU SAW ME BARE.

BUT YOU DIDN'T UNDERSTAND WHO
YOU WERE HOLDING IN YOUR PALMS.
YOU KNEW MY LIGHT.
IT WAS A MIRROR OF WHERE YOU CAME FROM.
IT FELT LIKE HOME TO HOLD ME.
YOU SPUN ME INTO CONFUSION
IN HOPES TO KEEP ME HIDDEN FROM THE TRUTH.
BUT YOU DIDN'T KNOW I WAS ALREADY HIDDEN IN HIM.

SO WHEN THE PRESSURE BECAME HONEST
AND HEAT TURNED TO FIRE-
YOU POPPED WORMWOOD.
YOU TURNED TO GHOST AND PLAYED THE VICTIM,
BECAUSE THAT'S WHAT YOU DO
WHEN THE LIGHT BECOMES SO BRIGHT.

I STUDY YOU
IN FROZEN MOMENTS
LIKE THE STORY IN MY MIND
PIECES ME TO YOU.

AS THOUGH I AM THERE,
NOT HERE,

MISSING YOU.

I FEEL YOU IN TENDER MOMENTS,
AS THOUGH THE DETAILS OF BEING
CARRY AN ESSENCE OF YOU.

THAT THE TREES SPEAK YOUR NAME
AND THE SOIL MISSES YOUR FEET.
YOUR WILD HAIR. YOUR WILD HEART.

BUT EVERYONE MISSES SOMEONE.

NOTICE, HOW YOU ARE MOON.

THE WAY YOU BLOOM IN PHASES.

YOU THOUGHT IT WAS BRAVE
TO DANCE IN MY STORM.
THAT THIS LIGHTENING UNDER YOUR SKIN
WOULD BLOOM INTO FEATHERS
FREEING YOU FROM THE WALLS YOU'VE BUILT.

THAT MY STORM
COULD BREAK YOU OPEN
IN SOME WAY HELPING YOU
REBUILD SOMETHING.

BELOVED, PAUSE.

LET'S TAKE THESE WALLS
AND CREATE CASTLES OF REFUGE
WITH DOORS THAT OPEN AND CLOSE.

MY STORM ISN'T TO WRECK YOUR WALLS
BUT MAKE A SANCTUARY THAT KEEP IN AND LET OUT.

SUCH VACANT COMPANY.
     LOOK WHAT OBLIGATION HAS DONE.

YOU'VE BECOME WEATHER.
TODAY A RAINFALL,
TOMORROW THE SUN.
YOU'VE BECOME WEATHER.
DROUGHT TO MY HEART.
NEXT DAY A FLOOD.
I ASK FOR CLEAR SKIES,
A SUNRISE
AND LIKE THE WEATHER
CONTROL- I HAVE NONE.

WHY IS HOLDING SO NATURAL.
THE WAY FIST DRAW IN.
THE WAY THINGS FIT TOGETHER.
LIKE YOU AND I
IN THE DESERT OF MY MIND.

I AM PARCHED, DRIED UP AND TIRED.
LIKE YOU IN THE DESERT OF MY MIND.

DON'T BE DECIEVED,
EXPECTATION IS A CEILING.

THIEVERY OF LOVE. BINDER OF DREAMS.
FIRE DIMMER, NO ROOM TO BREATHE.

IF I PIN YOU ON MY VISION BOARD TO FIT WHAT I EXPECT,
I WILL BE DISAPPOINTED EVERYTIME.

BUT IF I LAY YOU IN MY OPEN HAND WITH COMPASSION-
EVERY LIMITATION IS TRANSCENDED
BY GRACE.

ON THE OTHER SIDE, WE MUST ACKNOWLEDGE THE ELEMENT
OF RESPONSIBILTIY. IF YOU SHOW UP AND PRESENT
YOURSELF ONE WAY GROOMING SOMEONE TO BELIEVE IN THIS
IDEATION OF YOU...THEN WHEN THE LIGHT EXPOSES YOU-
REDIRECT BY GASLIGHTING THE CONCEPT OF EXPECTATION
EVEN THOUGH IT WAS YOU WHO DID NOT WALK THE TALK...
TAKE ACCOUNTABILITY FOR WHAT YOU PUT OUT THERE. TAKE
RESPONSIBILITY FOR THE GARDENS YOU STARTED,
THE CANVASES YOU BEGAN AND THE LANGUAGE
THAT DRIPS FROM YOUR TONGUE.

THERE IS ALWAYS GRACE, UNMERITED LOVE.
DON'T RUSH IN. DON'T RUSH OUT. GIVE TIME TIME.
NEEDING CLOSURE IS AN ILLUSION. WE ALL STAND ON BOTH
SIDES OF THE EXPECTATIOON EQUATION. TAKE A BREATH.
WHAT CAN YOU CLEAR UP? WHAT CAN YOU RELEASE?

DID YOU KNOW COLLABORATION
IS AN ESSENCE OF LIGHT.
IT'S THE MOON THAT REFLECTS THE
SUN'S LIGHT INTO THE NIGHT. WHY
WOULDN'T WE
REFLECT ONE ANOTHER
TO ILLUMINATE
SOMEONE ELSE'S DARK?

YOU BE SUN. I'LL BE MOON.

IN THIS SKY-
THERE IS ENOUGH ROOM.

YOU'VE BECOME
MY PLANETARY
ENABLER.
HOLDING UP
MY HOPE
AND BAROMETERS.
YOU'VE BECOME
SOMETHING
THAT CAN TAKE
EVERYTHING
FROM ME.

HOW I'VE WRAPPED
MYSELF SO IN YOU
THAT I'D RATHER BE
PART OF YOU
THAN A GALAXY
OF MY OWN.

SOMETIMES IT'S SIMPLE.
SOMETIMES IT'S AN ART OF BEING GENTLE.
I FIND SUCH STRENGTH IN MY SOFT.
IN THE WAY I LOOK FOR GRACE
IN QUIET SPACES OF DARK.
THE WAY I'VE ALWAYS BEEN
MORE MOON THAN SUN.

YES, YOU STRANGER.
HAVE BECOME MY ANCHOR.

LOVE IN THREE WORDS:
    COZY.
        COFFEE.
            POETRY.

LET ME LIGHT YOUR DARK.
THESE CANDLES ARE BUILT BY WAX AND OPEN PALMS,
THE LIGHT IGNITED BY VULNERABLE CALM.
YOU THINK THESE MOUNTAINS CAME EASY
BUT YOU DIDN'T SEE THE CAVES I SLEPT IN,
THE WATERFALLS THAT BAPTIZED ME.
YOU SEE ONLY THIS MOUNTAIN, A LADDER LIFTING LIGHT-
BUT PLEASE BELIEVE WE ALL HAVE DARK VALLEYS AND NIGHT
AND I WOULDN'T STAND HERE, WITH A TORCH IN MY HAND- FI
FROM MY HEART. VEINS THAT WERE ONCE UNZIPPED BY ALL T
STORIES, THE HERITAGE OF PAIN.
IT'S REAL TO FEEL. IT'S OKAY TO HEAL.

LET ME LIGHT YOUR DARK, I SAID.
PEEL OPEN AND PEER, LIKE FIREFLIES APPEAR.
I SEE YOU. HAUNTING HUMAN WE ARE.
LET ME LIGHT YOUR DARK AND DRINK
FROM THE GLASS OF I GET YOU, I FEEL THAT, I KNOW.
THE WAY WE LAY DOWN OUR WEAPONS
THERE REALLY IS NO DIFFERENCE BETWEEN US-
NO SKIN, DOLLARS, QUALITIES.
SAME HANDS, SAME BRUISED KNEES.
LET ME LIGHT YOUR DARK.

AND FOR EVERY TORCH PASSED ON, WE ARE WARRIORS OF
HEALING. I'LL TEACH YOU MY STRONG - SO LONG AS YOU
PROMISE ME THAT THE NEXT TIME YOU BELIEVE YOUR DARK IS
TOO MUCH OR TOO BIG, PAUSE AND REMEMBER- THE WAY OUR
SOLAR SYSTEM HOLDS ITSELF UP AND THE SKY DOESN'T FALL
DOWN. AND EVEN IN THE BLANKETS OF OUR GALAXY THERE AR
CONSTELLATIONS OF YOU AND CONSTELLATIONS OF ME.
AND IF THAT IS NOT ENOUGH PAUSE AND RECALL THE WEIGHT
THE GROUND AND WHETHER YOU ARE PLANTED OR BURRIED TIN
WILL ALWAYS PULL YOU TOWARD THE LIGHT.

PLEASE, LET ME LIGHT YOUR DARK. YOU SEE THIS SHADOW IS
NOT HAUNTING ME, THIS SHADOW JUST CREATES SPACE FOR
SHARED VULNERABILITY. AND I UNDERSTAND THIS SHADOW,
THIS SHADOW WILL ALWAYS BE. BECAUSE, I, YOU, WE, CHOOS
TO STAND IN THE LIGHT.

STRANGEST PAIN.
HOW YOU TAKE UP ALL THE SPACE
AND NO SPACE AT THE SAME TIME.

I KNOW YOU DIDN'T SEE IT
BECAUSE YOU DIDN'T GRIEVE IT
SO I WILL TUCK IT INTO
POCKETS FOR IT TO HIDE.
UNTIL YOU INVITE ME IN YOUR SWIMMING POOL
CORUSCATING AND REFLECTING WHAT I THOUGHT
WAS REAL AND WISE.
BUT NOW WE'RE DROWNING AND WE'RE DYING
IN THIS OCEAN FROM YOUR LYING
AND BEING WASHED UP ONTO BEACHES
BRUISED AND PARALYZED.
SO YOU CALL IT GLOBAL WARMING
WHEN ALL IT IS IS ROTTING
AND THIS CYCLE REPEATS FOR LIFETIMES.

WHAT IF I TOLD YOU THERE ARE CITIES
IN THE VEINS OF YOUR UNFOLDING
WITH ROADS THAT REVEAL
THE UNKNOWING.
AND I AM TRYING TO FIGURE OUT
TO TAKE WHAT I THOUGHT WAS BROKEN
AND SEE IT AS I'VE OPENED FROM THE INSIDE.
THAT MY GUTS MAY BE SPILLING
BUT YOUR ENERGY EATS FROM IT
SO EXHALE IT INTO SACRIFICE.

BUT THIS ISN'T FOR YOU.
IT'S FOR ME TO RELEASE SOME BLEEDING,
LET GO OF THE CONSUMING SO
I DON'T PASS THIS BEYOND ME AND YOU.
SO I GET THAT YOU WE'RE GRIEVING
BUT I'VE BEEN LEARNING YOU'VE BEEN TEACHING ME
TO HEAL BY MY OWN RIGHT.
AND ALL THE PETALS THAT YOU'VE PLUCKED AND
HAVE KEPT FOR GOOD LUCK
I HOPE THEY BLESS YOU WITH LIGHT AND LOVE.

OR BURN YOU WITH INTENTION, RIP YOU FROM ANY
MENTION OF ME. I AM ENOUGH.

YOU TAUGHT ME HOW TO GROW
UNDER MY OWN MOON.
PLANTING SEEDS IN SACRED PLACES
BUT HAVING NO INTENTION
TO SEE THEM BLOOM.

I MELT THE MOON,
AND DRINK HER LIGHT.

LEAVE ENOUGH SPACE
FOR THE SUN TO BLESS YOU.

OPEN FIELDS.
OPEN PALMS.
OPEN TRUST.

I SEE WHAT YOU ARE,
SHAPE SHIFTER YOU.

YOUR MAGIC TONGUE MAY BE
SHAPED LIKE THE MOON,
BUT THAT'S BECAUSE NO ONE
STUDIES THE DARKNESS
LIKE YOU.

CAN YOU POUR
YOUR HEARTACHE
INTO MY PALMS.

THESE LINES ARE STREAMS
OF SALT AND LIGHT.

THE WARMTH A SHELTER.
AND WE CAN HEAL
WITH THE HEARTBEAT FOUND
IN THE EARTH OF ME
AND THE EARTH OF YOU.

OUR ANCHOR HAS A WEAK ROPE.

AS I SINK,
I SEE MY LIFE BOAT FLOAT
INTO THE DISTANCE.

IT IS EXHAUSTING TO REACH FOR YOU AS I SINK.
ITS EXHAUSTING TO NEED YOU, SO I SINK.

IT WAS RAIN
THAT RAISED ME.
WHERE I LEARNED
TO DRINK RATHER
THAN DROWN.

THEY WILL TURN YOUR CONFIDENCE
INTO INCENSE
AND NOURISH THEIR HUNGER
WITH YOUR ASHES.

THEY WILL ASK YOU
TO FORGET YOURSELF.
TO FORGET YOU HAVE
SO MUCH REASON TO RISE.

IT DIDN'T BREAK YOU
IT OPENED YOU.

THIS PRACTICE-

MAY IT BE THE WILDERNESS
WHERE YOUR FLOWERS
BLOOM INTO FEATHERS.

WHERE RAGE IS THE CATALYST
AND PAIN NO LONGER SHAPES YOU,
BUT SHIFTS YOU.

I BROKE YOU LIKE A PROMISE.

LET YOU GO, JUST LIKE YOU WANTED.

MY LOVE IS THE RIVER THAT CHANGED YOU.
THAT WORE YOUR ROCKS INTO SEDIMENT.
THAT SUNK YOU TO THE CENTER.
OPENED YOU, FROM THE EARTH OF MY RIVER.

MAY YOUR PRISONS NO LONGER BE COFFINS,
BUT COCOONS.

**HOW ARE YOU ALLOWING CHANGE TO CHANGE YOU?
MAKE THE LISTS HERE.
WHAT NEEDS TO GO? WHAT NEEDS TO STAY?
ALLOW CHANGE TO CHANGE YOU.**

YOUR WIND GIVES WEIGHT. I OPEN.
YOUR LIGHT GIVES HEAT. I BLOOM.
YOUR LOVE GIVES. GRACE. I GROW.
YOUR SEASONS CHANGE, SO I MOVE.

**ALLOW CHANGE TO CHANGE YOU.**

I WISH I KNEW THE STORIES
AND THE LANGUAGE OF THEIR PAIN.
THE PATH IT TOOK
AND HOW IT CHANGED OUR NAME.
THE VALLEYS IT TOOK
TO BUILD THE MOUNTAINS WE ARE.
A WELL WITHIN US,
BURIED DEEP DOWN FAR.

I WANT TO UNCOVER,
THE QUIET MOMENTS
THEY HAD UNDER THE MOON.
WHAT DROVE THEIR CHOICES,
TO DO WHAT THEY DO.

I WANT TO EAT FROM THE HANDS
THEY TOOK REFUGE IN.
THE COURAGE IT TOOK
TO BEGIN AGAIN.
I WANT TO BECOME THE BREATH
THAT SURVIVED THE RAIN.
WITH GENTLE INTENSITY,
THEIR WILL MAINTAINED.

I AM OVER THE MOUNTAIN.
I AM THEIR SOMEDAY.
I AM PETALS BORN FROM BLOOD.
I AM PETALS BORN FROM HATE.
I AM RITUAL, PRAYER, A RIOT AWAKE,
FULL BODY STRETCH UNABLE TO BREAK.
POWER, KNOWING AND ALL THE ABOVE
IS DERIVED FROM MY ARMENIAN BLOOD.

IN THE EARTH OF YOU,
AFTER THE EXHALE,


WITHIN THE HEART
OF YOUR PAUSE


LIVES THE STEADY
AND THE STILL.

AS I SOFTEN THESE EDGES,
THE MAZE I'VE BEEN WANDERING
BEGINS TO FOLD OVER
INTO WAVES WITH A HORIZON.

AS I SOFTEN THESE EDGES,
THE HAND CUFFS BLOOM INTO OPTIONS-
INTO CHOICES AND CHOOSING.

AS I SOSFTEN THESE EDGES,
I GO FROM WALLS AND DEAD ENDS TO
BREATHE IN, BREATHE OUT, BEGIN AGAIN.

THINGS DON'T JUST SLIP AWAY.
IT'S YOUR EFFORT IN THE GRIP.
RESILIENCE WITH THE HIT.
IF YOU COME BACK,
TO WATER IT.

DON'T MAKE YOURSELF
AN AFTER THOUGHT.

YOU ARE THE LINING
HOLDING OUR STORIES INTO PLACE.
YOU ARE THE MOON RELIEVING THIS WEIGHT.

DO NOT MAKE YOURSELF
AN AFTER THOUGHT.

AS THOUGH THE MOON DIDN'T BIRTH YOU
AND THE FLAME DIDN'T CHANGE YOU.
AS THOUGH YOU DIDN'T TREK MOUNTAINS
DRINKING HOPE FROM THE SUN.
MILES OF MAKING
FROM THE UNDONE WE BECOME.

YOUR LOVE IS AN ORACLE
CONSTRUCTED BY GRACE.

YOU ARE THE LINING
HOLDING OUR STORIES INTO PLACE.

AS YOU BURY YOUR FEET INTO THE SHORELINE
OF INQUIRY WATCH HOW EACH WAVE
BECOMES CURRICULUM. HOW YOU BECOME A
STUDENT OF YOUR OWN ANCHORAGE.
AN ARTIST OF YOUR OWN REFUGE.

A STUDENT. AN ARTIST. CAN YOU PARTICIPATE IN THE LANDSCAPE OF NOTICE?

THESE PIECES BUILD THE TRUTH OF OUR INTERIOR WORLD THAT GUIDE AND DIRECT ALL THE CHOICE WE MAKE. WE MUST LEARN TO ADAPT AND EXPLORE. WHAT IS THE WHY BEHIND YOUR WHY.

ALLOW YOUR PRACITCE TO TAKE YOU HERE.
EVERY FORWRAD FOLD, GO IN.
BE OPEN, BE BREATH.
THIS PRACTICE IS A CONDUIT OF THE UNFOLDING.
SACRED GEOMETRY
WRAPPED IN SKIN AND LOVE.

THE EDGES AND YOUR RIPTIDE.
THE MANY MILES I HAVE GONE,
MOVING ME NOWHERE.

YOUR RIPTIDE. MANY MILES.
IN THIS RIPTIDE.

YOU CONFUSE THE WEEDS
WITH STRANGLING.

NOT SEEING HOW THEY CRAWL
UP FROM THE DARK,
ASKING TO BE HEALED.

THAT ALL THINGS HOLD
AN EXPIRATION DATE.

EVEN YOUR OLD WOUNDS AND WAYS
COME UP FOR AIR.

YOU SAID I WAS TOO MUCH.
AND THAT IS FINE,

BECAUSE I KNOW WHOLENESS
IS FOREIGN TO YOU.

NEVER ENOUGH INK TO MAKE SENSE OF YOU.
NEVER ENOUGH EXHALES TO RID YOU.

SO I TAKE IT FROM BESIDE ME,
MOVE IT TO BEHIND ME.
TURNING SOMETHING OLD
TO SOMETHING NEW.

BECAUSE CLOSURE SEES NO ESCAPE.
IT DECORATES THE HEARTACHE,
ORCHESTRATES THE LONG WAIT.
A CYCLE I CHOOSE TO BREAK.

MOVE IT FROM BESIDE ME,
GROW FROM WHAT'S BEHIND ME.

RAISE ME
WITH YOUR
RAINWATER.

I LOVE
HOW BEAUTIFUL
YOU STORM.

1825 SUNSETS SINCE YOU.
AND I KEEP TRYING TO
GET BACK AND BACK TO YOU.
I CHASE THE LIGHT
HOPING IT WILL LEAD
TO THE SUNRISE
THAT I NEED.

-FIVE YEARS

YOU BURN ME IN CIRCLE
SCOLDING AND UNFOLDING
INTO STRANGER

EACH MOUNTAIN I USE TO KNOW
HOLDING MY BACKBONE IN PLACE
CRUMBLING AWAY

REFUGE INTO RELIEF
OF BLOOD BUBBLING ONTO SKIN
I CAN'T HELP YOU. YOU WON'T LET ME
YOU CAN'T HELP ME. YOU WON'T LET ME

GRACE IS
HONORING
THE PACE
THE SPACE
AND ALL THE WAYS
YOU TURN RAIN
INTO FLOWER PETALS.

VITALITY IS THE AUTHOR OF JOY.
SPACE IS THE HEALER OF PAIN.
THE ONLY WITNESS TO BELIEF
IS ACTION. THE ONLY TEACHER
IS THAT OF GRACE.

WHAT DO YOU NEED TO PLUG IN?
WHERE DO YOU FEEL MOST SPACIOUS?
LIST IT OUT. FILL THIS PAGE WITH THE
THINGS YOU NEED FOR REFUGE, TO
RESTORE, TO RECOVER AND UNCOVER.
COME HERE OFTEN.

THE SAME WAY SEEDS FALL
AND CREATE SOMETHING NEW.
MISTAKES ARE REDIRECTION
BACK TO YOU. -GRACE

I KEEP ALLOWING YOUR ARROWS
TO BLOOM IN ME.

NOT KNOWING THE DIFFERENCE
BETWEEN PLANTING AND
STABBING.

**HOW DO YOU SOFTEN YOUR EDGES?**

CULTIVATE THE DISCIPLINE
THAT DISSOLVES GRACE INTO THE
PATTERN OF YOUR PRACTICE.

**HOW DO YOU SOFTEN YOUR EDGES?**

PRACTICES:

- DIFFUSE YOUR FAVORITE OIL.
- GIVE SPACE AND BUFFER TIME BETWEEN WHAT YOU SCHEDULE.
- SURROUND YOURSELF WITH NATURAL LIGHTING AND PLANTS.
- DRESS COMFORTABLY.
- USE YOUR FAVORITE PEN.
- MAKE TIME FOR TEA.
- PRAY.
- WRAP YOURSELF IN SOFT, COZY BLANKETS.
- HONOR THE HUMAN YOU ARE.
- STRETCH OFTEN.
- BURN YOUR FAVORITE CANDLE.
- SET THE SPACE, THE TONE, THE FEEL.

## HOW DO YOU SOFTEN YOUR EDGES?

PETALS FOR PERMISSION, GEMS FOR GRACE:

- YOU DO NOT KNOW WHAT YOU DO NOT KNOW.
- YOU ARE ONLY ONE PERSON CARRYING SO MUCH.
- DO ONE THING AT A TIME.
- PARENT THE NARRATIVES, DON'T LET EGO DRIVE THE DEFAULT- WITNESS IT. NEGOTIATE WITH IT.
- JUST BECAUSE IT FEELS REAL, DOES NOT MEAN IT IS TRUE.
- MEET YOURSELF WHERE YOU ARE.
- GIVE YOURSELF PERMISSION TO NOT KNOW ALL THE ANSWERS.
- BE INTENTIONAL.
- YOU DO NOT HAVE TO TALK OR EXPLAIN OR COMPENSATE FOR ANYTHING- YOU HAVE NOTHING TO PROVE.
- TRUST THE TIMING OF YOUR LIFE- NOTHING BLOOMS ALL YEAR LONG.

THIS IS YOUR WELCOME. YOUR CALL TO NOURISH, SHOW UP AND RECONCILE THE ART OF YOU. A MAP INTO WHO YOU ARE AND THE GRACE TO ALLOW TRAILS AND TRIALS TO UNFOLD AT PACE TRUSTING IN PROVIDENTIAL CARE. THE TIMING IS NOW. THIS IS A MAGICAL MOVEMENT OF BREATH AND LOVE AND SUPPORT. BE HERE. WITH KINDNESS. WITH GRACE. WITH LOVE. LET THIS WORK BE YOUR PRAYER, YOUR MINISTRY.

**MY PRACTICE LOOKS LIKE...**

**MY PRACTICE FEELS LIKE...**

**IT'S YOUR PRACTICE.
YOU ARE MOVING POETRY.
YOUR BREATH, CADENCE.
AS YOU PRACTICE,
YOU BECOME THE POEM.**

I WOULD POSSESS YOU IN PIECES
BECAUSE I TRUST IN THE PROCESS LIKE
PUZZLES KNOWING IN TIME IT ALL FITS.

I WOULD HOLD YOU LIKE CONVERSATIONS IN
LONG CAR RIDES
BECAUSE SPACE IS ALL WE HAVE TO FILL.

I WOULD WRAP YOU IN COZY BLANKETS
LIKE I DO WITH QUIET MORNING MOMENTS
SAVORING THE TASTE OF
PRODUCTIVITY AND COFFEE.

I WOULD CARVE YOU INTO THE TREE OF MY
HEART BECUASE THERE IS SOMETHING I LIKE
ABOUT THE ACHE YOU LEAVE.
AND I KNOW THAT EVERY SCAR WILL BIRTH A
SEED.

I WOULD STRETCH YOU INTO MY PRACTICE
INVITING ALL VITALITY, HOLD AND SOFT.
SO WHOLE, I BREATHE-
YOU, MY EXHALE, SOFT RELIEF.

DEAR LOVE,

YOU ARE COCOON
ACAPELLA AND HONEYMOON.

OH LOVE,

YOU ARE COCOON
SUFFOCATING AND DOOM,

HOARDING LOVE DOES NOT
HEAL LOVE.
IT REVOKES THE BREATH,
THE REFUGE,
THE SOFT.

AND SHACKLES LOVE INTO A
SMALL WOODEN BOX.

PACKED WITH SHATTERED
WINDOWS AND SHAME.

IT'S SIMPLE MATH-

HOARDING LOVE
GIVES BIRTH
TO PAIN.

SHE DOESN'T CALL DAY SUN,
ONLY "IT'S HIDING".

HER EYES HAVE TASTE FOR THINGS
THAT SHINE IN THE DARK.
IN TODDLER TELLING,
SHE BURSTS IN JOY
AS THOUGH HER HEART FEEDS
FROM IT.

THIS CHILD, FULL MOON.
FULL HEART, FULL BREATH.

AN EXHALE TO EVERY COLD NIGHT.

YOU DO NOT KNOW WHAT
YOU ARE ASKING ME.

TO TURN OFF MY HEART AS
THOUGH YOURS DOESN'T
PUMP LIFE THROUGH YOU.

NOURISHING IS BEAUTIFUL.
WHAT IS BEAUTIFUL IS NOURISHING.

MY PHOENIX WAS BORN FROM A FOREST FIRE.

ALL THAT HAD TO BURN TO CREATE
THE BRILLIANCE OF THIS.

YOU ARE THE UNDERCURRENT
RAILING I REACH FOR

WHEN THE WAVES
BECOME A STORM
AND ALL THE WORLD IS DROWNING-
I REACH TO YOU FOR WARMTH.

AS GRAVEL ROADS GROW DISTANCE
NO MATTER THE PLASTIC TOWN
NO MATTER AGE, NUMEROUS DAYS
I REMAIN NOT LOST BUT FOUND.

- HOME

I WOULD TURN ALL YOUR
CANVASES TO WATERCOLOR.
BECAUSE ME DROWNING
IS ART TO YOU.

YOUR GHOST IS AN OCEAN.




AND YOU LEFT ME WANDERING YOUR BEACHES.

YOU ASK ME HOW TO WRITE POETRY.
AND I LOOK AT YOUR FINGERS THINKING
WHETHER THEY MAKE OR HOLD.

BECAUSE IF THEY MAKE-
I KNOW THEY WILL CREATE AND DEMAND
THE TRUTH OF LIFE TO UNFOLD FROM
THE BLOOMING OF YOUR BRAIN.

BUT IF THEY HOLD-
I KNOW YOU CAN REALLY ONLY FEEL
AND THAT SOMETIMES IT IS BETTER
TO SINK AND NOT KNOW
HOW TO CONVEY THE SINKING.

BECAUSE EVERY FEELING HOLDS AN ANCHOR
MADE OUT OF SENTENCES,
AND EVERY HEARTBREAK BURNS INTO
THE SAME DUST OF BUTTERFLY WINGS.
FRAGILE, REAL AND EVER SO FERTILE.

SO WHETHER YOU MAKE OR HOLD-
I KNOW YOU'D TAKE THE BROKEN PIECES
TO PLANT THEM INTO THE COFFIN
OF YESTERDAY DIFFERENTLY.

THAT YOU'D YEILD HOPE AND INFINITY OF NOW.
YOU ASK ME HOW TO WRITE POETRY? OPEN
YOUR HEART BECAUSE LIFE
WILL TEACH YOU HOW.

DARLING, I CAN TEACH YOU
TO TURN
PEOPLE,
PLACES
AND PAIN
INTO AN EXHALE.

NO NEW MOONS,
HOW YOU'VE MADE A
GRAVEYARD OUT OF MEMORY.
SPLINTERS IN EVERY WORD
I SAY AS YOU SKIP STONES
ACROSS MY BOUNDARIES.

HOW QUICK YOU WENT FROM
SOMETHNIG TO EVERYTHING.

WE WERE ALL AT ONE TIME
A SILHOUETTE TO SOMEONE.

THAT NO MATTER HOW BRIHGT
THEY SHINE, THEY WOULD
NEVER BE OUR SHADE OF LIGHT.

IT'S LIFE, YOU'LL BE FINE.

LET THIS MEAN SOMETHING-
          YOU OPENED TO GO FORTH.

SWEATING PRAYERS
          INTO LOTUS FLOWERS.

YOU'VE WORKED, NURSING
          NOTHING INTO SOMETHING,

POUR YOURSELF INTO ME.
THE WAY DAYLIGHT SPILLS
THROUGH CLOSED WINDOWS.

GROWING WINGS ARE BORN
FROM BROKEN BOOKS. EVERY
MAP THAT MAKES NO SENSE.
HOW THE STRETCH FEELS MORE
LIKE A YAWN AND I PINCH
MYSELF TO BREATHE. HOW
THERE ARE NEVER ENOUGH
EXHALES TO RID YOU.

YOU ARE THE RIPPED OUT PAGES
FROM MY STORY. I MISS THE WAY
YOU WROTE ALL OVER MY SOUL

BELIEVE IN YOUR SUNRISE.


THAT THE SKY WAITS FOR YOUR LIGHT.

DON'T DILUTE SOMETHING
FOR THE ILLUSION TO FEEL FULL.
I BELIEVE IN YOUR MOON.
I'LL WAIT WITH YOU.
THROUGH EVERY PHASE.
YOU DON'T EVEN NEED TO BE FULL,
TO BE WHOLE.

THOSE CRACKS THAT YOU THOUGHT
MEANT YOU WERE BROKEN,

ARE ACTUALLY DOORS
YOUR HEALING HAS OPENED.

# SELF CARE AS AN ACTIVE ART

I TAKE SELF LOVE SO SERIOUS BECAUSE I HAVE WITNESSED AGAIN AND AGAIN THAT WHEN I AM NOT FULL WITHIN, I CANNOT OFFER OR EXTEND TO OTHERS. I SEE IT WITH STUDENTS, CLIENTS AND COMMUNITY. WHEN WE DO NOT FEEL COMFORTABLE IN OUR SKIN, IT CHALLENGES OUR ABILITY TO CREATE A WELCOMING AND WARM SPACE FOR OTHERS. WHEN WE ARE CRITICAL AND HARD ON OURSELVES, WE TEND TO BE CRITICAL AND HARD ON EVERYTHING.

WHEN WE ARE SMITTEN FOR THE PRESENT MOMENT AND THANKFUL FOR THE NOW, ABUNDANT LOVE THREADS ITSELF INTO EVERY BREATH, IN EVERY SMILE SHARED AND EVERY MOMENT EXPERIENCED. WHEN GIVEN FROM A PLACE OF HAVE, A PLACE OF COMPLETE- LIGHT SHINES INTO THE CRACKS AND THINGS BEGIN TO GROW, FLOURISH AND OPEN.

THE GREATEST COMMANDMENT IN THE BIBLE IS TO LOVE THE LORD WITH ALL YOUR HEART AND ALL YOUR SOUL (MATTHEW 22:37-40). THE SECOND IS TO LOVE YOUR NEIGHBOR AS YOURSELF. LOVE IS EVERYTHING. THE FOUNDATION ON HOW WE LOVE OTHERS IS DEPENDENT UPON HOW WE LOVE OURSELVES. ALLOW THESE JOURNALING AND INQUIRY PRACTICES TO SERVE AS A SACRED INVITATION BACK HOME. A LOVE LETTER BACK TO YOU.

I FEEL KINDEST TO MYSELF WHEN...

WHAT WORDS COMFORT ME THE MOST?

**LIST YOUR FAVORITE AFFIRMATIONS HERE:**

**LIST YOUR FAVORITE SONG LYRICS HERE:**

**LIST YOUR FAVORITE QUOTES HERE:**

# DOG EARED THOUGHTS

# DOG EARED THOUGHTS

# DOG EARED THOUGHTS

www.ingramcontent.com/pod-product-compliance
Lightning Source LLC
Chambersburg PA
CBHW050804160426
43192CB00010B/1640